Dog Separation Anxiety

How To Treat And Prevent Separation Anxiety In Dogs

Bruno Michael

Your Free Gift

As a way of thanking you for the purchase, I'd like to offer you a complimentary gift:

- **5 Pillar Life Transformation Checklist:** This short book is about life transformation, presented in bit size pieces for easy implementation. I believe that without such a checklist, you are likely to have a hard time implementing anything in this book and any other thing you set out to do religiously and sticking to it for the long haul. It doesn't matter whether your goals relate to weight loss, relationships, personal finance, investing, personal development, improving communication in your family, your overall health, finances, improving your sex life, resolving issues in your relationship, fighting PMS successfully, investing, running a successful business, traveling etc. With a checklist like this one, you can bet that anything you do will seem a lot easier to implement until the end. Therefore, even if you don't continue reading this book, at least read the one thing that will help you in every other aspect of your life. Grab your copy now by clicking/tapping here or simply enter http://bit.ly/2fantonfreebie into your browser. Your life will never be the same again (if you implement what's in this book), I promise.

PS: I'd like your feedback. If you are happy with this book, please leave a review on Amazon.

Introduction

Have you had the misfortune of walking into your house, which you keep in pristine condition at all times, only to find everything topsy-turvy? The furniture is all over the place, not to mention overturned; your door frames have deep claw marks, window sills have bloodstained teeth marks and your answering machine has about 90 messages from neighbors raising hell over your dog's howls and endless barking?

If so, then you do not need too deep an introduction to separation anxiety… you've experienced it first hand, and know how unpleasant it can be. "Separation anxiety" is a mild label for what is destructive, even distractive behavior.

Thirty years ago, this phrase was not too common in dog training circles. Today however, it is rare to find a dog owner who has not heard or experienced separation anxiety. More and more dog owners are seeking out as much information on the subject as they can find so they know what to do when faced with the problem.

This book is here to help, as it walks you through the subject. The first part will focus on what separation anxiety is (and is not), symptoms and misdiagnosis of the same. The second part will equip you with functional information on steps to take, both preventive and not, to thwart this destructive behavior. At the very end, you should be able to deal with any curveballs your dog throws you… figurative curveballs, of course.

How To Treat and Prevent Separation Anxiety In Dogs

Let's begin!

How To Treat and Prevent Separation Anxiety In Dogs

Table of Contents

Your Free Gift _____ 2

Introduction _____ 3

Part 1: Understanding & Diagnosing Separation Anxiety In Dogs _____ 8

Understanding The Separation Anxiety Phenomenon _____ 8

  Is It Natural That Separation Anxiety Should Kick In, In Dogs? _____ 8

  Separation Anxiety Stems From Real Stress, And Must Be Viewed As Such _____ 10

What Causes Separation Anxiety In Dogs? Understanding The Elements Responsible _____ 12

20 Most Common Symptoms Of Separation Anxiety _____ 19

Common False Positives You Should Know About 23

  Simulated Separation In Dogs _____ 26

Isolation Distress And Separation Anxiety: What's The Difference? _____ 27

Have A Look These Abstract Examples To Develop Better Understanding: _____ 27

Dog Breeds & Separation Anxiety: Dog Breeds Most Prone To Separation Anxiety _____ 29

Part 2: Preventing Separation Anxiety In Dogs Before It Sets In _____ 33

10 Potent Steps To Keep Separation Anxiety At Bay _____ 33

The Steps: _____ 34

Part 3: Effectively Treating Separation Anxiety In Dogs _____ 37

How Do I Help My Dog? The Four Options Of Treating Separation Anxiety _____ 37

Where Do I Start? Creating A Suitable Environment & Routine For Your Dog _____ 40

Rewards _____ 40

Buckling Down: Effective, Responsive Conditioning Measures To Cure Separation Anxiety In Your Dog _____ 46

Homeopathic And Herbal Remedies For Separation Anxiety In Your Dog _____ 62

Conclusion _____ 65

Do You Like My Book & Approach To Publishing? 66

   1: First, I'd Love It If You Leave a Review of This Book on Amazon. _____ 66

   2: Get Updates When I Publish New Books ___ 66

   3: Grab Some Freebies On Your Way Out; Giving Is Receiving, Right? _____ 67

Part 1: Understanding & Diagnosing Separation Anxiety In Dogs

Understanding The Separation Anxiety Phenomenon

In her phenomenal book, *"Clinical Behavioral Medicine for Small Animals"*; Dr. Karen Overall describes separation anxiety as being, *"a condition whereby animals display distinct symptoms of great anxiety or extreme distress, in those instances when they are left to their own devices."*

The most common symptoms of separation anxiety in dogs are inclusive of destructive behavior, soiling the house, and excessive vocalization (howling, barking, whining etc.). Many dogs suffering from separation anxiety will also refuse to eat and drink when they are left alone. They will not tolerate crating; they will pant and salivate excessively, especially when the distress really kicks in and they will go to extreme lengths to attempt to escape from what they view as oppressive confinement. Of course, the situation is compounded by the fact that they show complete disregard for injury/self-harm as well as damage and destruction to their immediate surroundings.

Is It Natural That Separation Anxiety Should Kick In, In Dogs?

Think about it for a bit: it is wholly natural for a young mammal to experience feelings of anxiety when it is separated from its mothers and its siblings; this is an adaptive mechanism of survival that has been passed down since the earliest days of the earth. A pup that is separated from its family will cry in distress, and this will enable its mom to find it easily and thus put it out of harm's way. The wild is a harsh place: even a full-grown canine that is left alone instantly sees its chances of death climb up. There are so many elements: starvation could kill the canine, since it has no pack to make the hunting process easier, or it could perish from attack, seeing as here are no partners to offer mutual protection. For this very reason, separation anxiety signs in puppies are natural and should be expected, if only to a degree.

Examining the previous paragraph; it is apparent that a dog's canine companions are of great importance. Without them, survival becomes harder. Thus, it greatly influences a dog's adaptability as a species that we are able to condition them into accepting to getting left alone at all. In fact, it can be said that we are lucky that the problems we face, with regard to separation anxiety, are not more severe than they typically are. Especially in today's world where it is more common than not to have the entire family out of the house for most hours of the day, and the dog left completely alone; things could be a lot worse.

In previous times; the society shaped up in ways that meant fewer dogs were left alone at home. Usually, mom stayed at home and tended to it while dad went off to grind and bring home the family bread. As such, dogs were less exposed to the sort of daily isolation which contributes to the destructive behavior of separation anxiety. This could also explain why back then, separation anxiety was an unfamiliar subject among most dog training circles.

Separation Anxiety Stems From Real Stress, And Must Be Viewed As Such

Separation anxiety in dogs will go beyond the once-in-a-while mournful whimper when you step out of the house, or the occasional mysterious appearance of a slipper under the dining table, once you get back. Unlike the spates of mischief that most dogs exhibit; behaviors of separation anxiety stem from genuine stress.

Most dogs that suffer from separation anxiety will try and stay close to their owners as much as possible. They will shadow them everywhere... they will get up and walk him or her from the bedroom to the kitchen and back. They will lie at the owner's feet when he or she is quickly checking the mail and rarely let them out of their sight. These dogs will rarely, if ever, opt to spend time outdoors alone; you will have to be with them; otherwise, they will stay home. As soon as you start preparing to leave, the anxiety will kick in, and they will start to show it. Most of these dogs –though certainly not all of them- will crave lots of physical contact from the owner. When you start to leave, in addition to elimination, destruction and excessive vocalizing; they will be restless to the point where they drool, pant a lot, shiver, shun all food and treats and become withdrawn. While the behavior will typically be displayed every time you leave, there may be times when it only occurs on selected departures, such as leaving for work, or when you leave the house after coming home from work. When you return, your dog will be very excited and aroused.

Separation anxiety may be prevented by making sure that puppies have scheduled time periods where they get to learn to spend some time alone, either in their crates or their beds. Some dogs may appear to suffer from separation anxiety, but are really only afraid to be alone because something bad happened to them while they were alone. For example, they may have been badly shaken by fireworks, storms, Etc.

What Causes Separation Anxiety In Dogs? Understanding The Elements Responsible

1. The usual suspects

The truth is that some dogs show more proneness to separation anxiety than others, and this makes sense since dogs mimic humans in that different dogs have different defined personas (some dogs are quieter and more brooding, some are more aggressive, some have a significantly more excitable personalities, Etc.)

With this said, it is unclear why some dogs tend to be more prone to separation anxiety. There is anecdotal evidence suggesting it is more common in shelter dogs; dogs that may have either been abandoned or lost an important person in their past. It is also true that some dog breeds may indeed be more prone to separation anxiety, especially those more-people oriented dog breeds.

Life changes may also trigger separation anxiety, with the inclusion of sudden schedule changes, moving to a new house or sudden absences of family members (it could be a divorce, a family death, a child attending college, a spouse moving to another town for work, Etc.)

Let us examine these:

- **Change of family or guardian**

When a dog is abandoned, given away to a new family/guardian or surrendered to a shelter; this can trigger separation anxiety development, as the dog is suddenly plucked away from people it adores and is used to, and thrust among unfamiliar people. With time, the separation anxiety may get full-blown, and destructive behavior and self-harm will soon follow.

- **Change in schedule**

Abrupt changes in schedule, at least with regard to when/how long the dog is left alone, may trigger separation anxiety development. For instance; if you have been working from home, and thus your dog is used to you spending all but a couple of hours with you; you can see why separation anxiety will develop if you suddenly start attending a regular 9 to 5 shift that has you spend many more hours away from your dog. Especially if you do not transition slowly into your 9 to 5 (something that, in all honesty, is difficult to visualize let alone do), chances of separation anxiety developing are high.

- **Change in residence**

A new residence will be unfamiliar to the dog. It will take time before familiarity is cultivated. Moving to a new residence may trigger development of separation anxiety.

- **Changes in household membership**

Dogs are quick to develop deep bonds with each family member. They also have long memories. The sudden absence of a family member, perhaps due to death or moving to a faraway place, will register in the dog. Separation anxiety may develop.

2. Causative elements of separation anxiety based on gender, development, attachment, familial setup Etc.

It has to be said that the elements included below are not necessarily unanimous in nature. They are observations made in most, but not all dogs. As we said earlier; dogs have distinct, personalized psyches, behavior patterns and response mechanisms. With this in mind, let us delve into the elements:

- Male dogs tend to have bigger issues with separation anxiety than female dogs do. This is not to say that female dogs will not be quick to develop separation anxiety, but it is apparent that male dogs -especially ones that have not been castrated- develop separation anxiety at a higher frequency. Male dogs that have not been castrated are restless by default, and being confined to a closed space, alone, will only make it worse.

- Your dog will be more likely to develop problems related to separation anxiety if he or she is used to sleeping in your bed, or lounging on the couch with you. This makes sense: the higher intimacy levels that your dog is used to will make it harder to deal with loneliness. On the other hand, a dog that has been trained to spend the bulk of its time in its crate, including sleeping hours, will have fewer issues as it is used to spending time by itself.

- The fewer the number of people in the household, the more probable it is that the dog will develop separation anxiety. A dog that lives with a single adult is more likely to develop separation anxiety than one that lives with an adult couple. A dog that lives with multiple adults will be less likely to develop separation anxiety problems, compared to the former. Dogs that live in a vibrant family with children in it will be the least affected by separation anxiety. The reasoning behind this is that the fewer people the dog has to develop a bond with, the more attached it gets to them and the harder it is impacted by their absences. It becomes way more emotionally dependent to them, and is much more devastated when they are not around. On the other hand, a dog in a vibrant family has a lot more people to bond with, and it is likely that when one person is not around; another person is. The gaps in attention and companionship are this felt less.

- Dogs that have been doing their thing; perhaps roaming freely in the streets or housed in a shelter with many other dogs, and are adopted when they are older will be more likely to develop separation anxiety. This is because they are more set in their ways than puppies are, and suddenly having to spend many hours alone will be that much more devastating. With dogs however, the general rule is that it is harder for older dogs to adapt to new factors, surroundings and patterns than it is for puppies. If you are interested in adopting an older dog, it will be likelier for him to develop separation anxiety no matter how well-trained he is.

- Dogs that have been exposed to people outside the home, as well as to a wide range of experiences between the ages of 5 to 10 months will be less likely to develop issues related to separation anxiety. If the puppy was regularly introduced to the outdoors and strangers, early in its development, then the feelings of loneliness are not quite so intense. Think about people who were kept away from other people since they were very young, and have grown up largely keeping to themselves and staying indoors. On the surface, it may appear that they should be less lonely as they are used to being alone. The truth however is that they feel the loneliness much more intensely than regular, social folk. They know they cannot expect regular releases that come with interactions, as they almost never happen. All they can expect is the same old dross, day in day out. It's the same with dogs. If your dog is used to regular outdoor ventures and meeting other people, it becomes easier for him to wait until he gets taken out. It will happen sooner or later anyway. If your dog is mostly closeted and confined, it becomes harder to sit out the hours alone as there's little hope of an adventure afterwards.

- It is possible for dogs that were perfectly fine with being alone, and for a long time as well, to develop severe separation anxiety issues. 99% of the time however, this only happens if a nasty experience happens to befall the dog when you are away. If you leave the water running and it floods the house, the dog will be traumatized by the experience. It will become much more wary of being left alone. If you have to leave for two weeks, and have to leave the dog with an obtuse caregiver who ties the dog in the laundry room and leaves him there for hours on end; the experience may change him forever. It is best to make sure that all conditions are ideal before you leave the house. Make sure the dog has access to food and water; ensure that the water taps are closed; that the treats are nearby, Etc. You want the dog to be as unperturbed as possible.

- There is abundant evidence that dogs that become excessively attached to their owners are more likely to develop separation anxiety issues. If your dog is used to you doing everything while having him by your side, he will never know how to cope with bouts of loneliness when you are away. Your absences, even ones that are very short, will be very deeply felt. Even when you leave a responsible caregiver to tend for him, separation anxiety may develop. As such, if you allow your dog to follow you from room to room and encourage him to display leaving and greeting behavior that is more overt in nature; he will develop anxiety more easily when you are not around.

So how do you know when the dog is exhibiting symptoms of separation anxiety? The next chapter will cover that.

20 Most Common Symptoms Of Separation Anxiety

You now know what separation anxiety is, as well as the full range of factors and elements that cause it. The next step in your education is to understand symptoms to look out for.

Dogs that suffer separation anxiety will vocalize, become destructive and even eliminate, beginning either at the time the owner is preparing to leave or just shortly after departure. They will also express themselves in other varied ways.

Here are 20 common separation anxiety symptoms to watch for:

1. Constant barking, howling and whining: This vocalization stems from deep distress on the dog's part. Your dog will bark endlessly while you are away, and pepper his barks with howls and loud whining. The dog's vocalization is more likely to grow in intensity the longer you are away from home, but this will usually happen if you are leaving him on his own for too long. Still, you should investigate properly before chalking off the dog's vocalization to separation anxiety. Barking when you are away may be either due to unfamiliar sounds of strangers, or other animals on the property.

2. Intense pacing and restlessness: Your dog will pace endlessly, and he will usually pause to either bark or

howl. Your dog will be flustered and restless, constantly changing positions and clawing at things.

3. Excessive salivation and panting: This is attributable to both the distress the dog is in, as well as its hyper activity. If the dog is clawing at things as well as barking and howling; his system will have him panting and salivating so as to cool down.

4. Scratching windows and doors (including digging at doors)

5. Escaping a room or crate: Your dog may feel confined or oppressed in his room or crate, in addition to feeling lonely. He may thus devote his efforts to escaping it.

6. Drooling

7. Destruction of property (furniture, sofas, pillows as well as eating plants): Destructive activity will often be focused on the owner possessions, or at the doors that the owner used to depart. If the dog is confined, he'll damage the doors of his cage or room. A lot of the time, this destructive behavior will occur just shortly after your departure. Some dogs will try to escape or even become extremely anxious when they are confined. Thus, destructive behavior or house soiling when the dog is locked in its crate, the basement, or the laundry room may be due to barrier or confinement anxiety, and associated attempts at escaping.

8. Vomiting

9. Urinating or defecating indoors: Also known as elimination. Dogs that go ahead and eliminate when the owner is at home are either not be properly house trained, or they may have some medical problem.

10. Coprophagia: This simply means the consumption of feces. Of course, it is highly likely your dog will be eating his own elimination, especially seeing as he's alone. The exception is if he is able to access your own poo.

11. Chewing stuff (especially those things you have touched recently; and your scent still lingers on.)

12. Dilated pupils

13. Jumping through windows (the windows could be open or closed)

14. Trying to eat through walls: This will be done in a bid to escape, especially if the dog has a bad case of barrier anxiety

15. The dog follows you literally everywhere, after you arrive from work

16. Sweating

17. Hiding or even crying when you reach for your keys or perhaps make other signs which indicate that you plan on leaving the house

18. Ignoring his food

19. Overly excited behavior or even submissive body language once you arrive home

20. Destroying doors as well as other points of entry

Common False Positives You Should Know About

It is important that you take your time before concluding that your canine has separation anxiety issues. This is because it is quite possible that the issue lies elsewhere, and your dog does not suffer from separation anxiety. Your dog could have an issue that is medical in nature, for instance. His odd, destructive behavior may be caused by a lack of ample exercise, inadequate training or quite simply boredom. This chapter will look at several problems that could masquerade as separation anxiety disorder.

1: Incontinence

This medical issue may be a symptom of present kidney disease in your dog. It could also be an indicator of UTI, diabetes as well as many other diseases. If your dog starts peeing in the house out of nowhere, check with your vet first before you attribute this behavior to separation anxiety disorder.

2: Side-effects of medication

If your fluffy companion is on any meds, he or she may exhibit traits that are usually attributable to separation anxiety disorder. Excessive salivation, relieving on the carpeting, a drop in appetite and even anxiety itself may well result from the effects of dog medication. Again, consult with your vet before you arrive at any conclusions.

3: "Submissive and/or excitement urination"

There are some dogs that pee during play-time, greetings, when there is physical contact or when you are reprimanding and punishing them. These dogs will display such submissive behavior as holding the tail low, rolling over and exposing the belly, flattening the ears back against the head, etc. In this case, the dog's body language is more an indicator of personality type as opposed to stress.

4: Urine marking

Some dogs infamously pee inside because they are following their natural instinct to scent mark. As you may know, dogs mark their scent by leaving little traces of pee on walls and other vertical structures. This is a lot more common when the dog is not neutered.

5: Youthful destruction

Young dogs have a destructive streak in them. If you have raised a dog from pup-level to adult stage, you know this to be true. Pups love to chew on stuff, scratch, dig at surfaces Etc. They will do so even when you are at home.

6: Boredom

Dogs require mental stimulation. A dog that remains alone and unmotivated will act out in a bid to find something to do. This type of behavior is not hinged on distress... it is hinged on boredom.

7: Inadequate house training

Dogs that pee inside may not be properly house-trained. You could say the same thing for dogs that poop inside the house. The distinction, with regard to pooping, is when the dog poops indoors after it has been outside. In this case, your dog is very likely anxiety-pooping.

It is true that the dog could have been extensively housetrained yet still poops and urinates indoors. If this is the case, then the housetraining may either have been erratic in frequency, or it involved punishment instead of treats. As such, the dog may have developed great anxiety in relieving in the presence of its owner, and will be unable to go even when it's outside in your company.

Simulated Separation In Dogs

Simulated separation anxiety is a false anxiety disorder. However, it has just about the same dog stress symptoms.

How do you tell the difference?

Unlike dogs suffering from actual separation anxiety disorder, dogs that simulate this behavior are usually not motivated by nervousness or fear. This is merely a learned, attention-seeking behavior.

For instance, if your furry friend truly wants to sleep in your bed but is disallowed to, he may start whining by your door or even pee in the hallway if you do not cave in. This may lead you to misdiagnose his behavior, which is attention-seeking and not rooted in actual distress, as being rooted in separation anxiety.

It is vital that you do not indulge your fur-ball when he or she exhibits destructive behavior. If you reward your dog after doing an unwanted or forbidden thing, then you've just empowered him/her in misbehaving. Dogs are a lot like kids: if your kid is walking around smashing windows, you do not want to reciprocate by handing him some ice cream. You need to stamp out the behavior. In the case of your dog, you require to temporarily withdraw your attention and let him/her know you are upset.

Isolation Distress And Separation Anxiety: What's The Difference?

Distress over being left to their devices isn't always a full blown separation anxiety issue. First, consider that your dog may suffer from mild distress to severe anxiety disorder. In the context of this chapter; "distress" points to a lower intensity in stress behavior when your pet is alone. "Anxiety" points to an extreme panic attack.

Distinguishing between "isolation" and "separation" is vital. Isolation distress will mean that your dog does not want to be left alone – any human being will do for company... just don't leave him alone with nobody close by.

True separation anxiety will mean that the dog is hyper bonded to a particular individual. Even when in ample human company, the dog will continue to display stress behavior if the person that it is hyper-bonded to is absent. The stress behavior will still persist when in company of other dogs.

Have A Look These Abstract Examples To Develop Better Understanding:

Josh, a Cardigan Corgi, suffers from low-moderate isolation distress. Josh hates to be left alone when he is outdoors. At first, Josh's owner hadn't caught onto this, and Josh managed to injure himself badly by falling off a wall onto some cement steps roughly 8 feet below. It was a bizarre accident that the owner attributed at first to an appetite for adventure mixed in with a dash of clumsiness. In truth, Josh was trying to reach him through a window. When Josh is indoors, his isolation distress is noticeably milder. Josh will briefly bark when left alone downstairs, but he'll calm down and settle soon enough.

Tommy, on the other, exhibits true separation distress. He's an 8 year old Aussie Shepherd and he's been through at least 5 different homes prior to joining his present family. As it sometimes happens with dogs that get rehomed multiple times, Josh attaches himself to one of her new humans, the tween boy Jesse in this case, completely and nearly instantly. If the entire family is lounging on the lawn and Jesse has to go to the house for some reason or other, Josh the dog, could care less the rest of the family is still with him on the lawn. He becomes ultra-vigilant, watching anxiously and struggling to be let to enter the house after Jesse. If Jesse is gone for a while, Josh will start to pee and dig, and his struggling to be let go will become very intense.

Dog Breeds & Separation Anxiety: Dog Breeds Most Prone To Separation Anxiety

You may be wondering: why does my dog exhibit separation anxiety while my neighbor's canine seems perfectly fine despite being left alone for longer? Perhaps, you are reading this book to prepare you for separation anxiety once you own a dog. Among numerous reasons, the dog's breed may be a factor in developing separation anxiety disorder.

Here are dog breeds that tend to be more likely to experience separation anxiety compared to others:

1: The Labrador Retriever

Usually, this dog is adorable and very companionable. Recently however, they have dipped in both temperament and health. This may be a reason why Labrador Retrievers are a lot more likely to suffer from separation anxiety, as well as other behavioral challenges. The Labrador, known popularly as "The Lab", is still the most popular family breed, and its disposition remains a relaxed one. However, these dogs are so social and extroverted that they struggle greatly if left alone for lengthy time periods.

2: The Border Collie

Border Collies are known for their great intelligence. As a matter of fact, they rank top with regard to dog smarts. Owing to this, they may become bored if not provided with ample mental stimulation. When the dog is alone, it is mentally stimulated the least. Collies are also very high-energy in nature. This means that they need to be amply stimulated physically as well. If you leave them alone for a significant time period, they will quickly become bored, and separation anxiety may set in.

3: The Cavalier King Charles Spaniel

The dogs are great companion dogs that have been bred primarily to enjoy spending lots of time with their human "parents". Leaving them alone for longer periods will trigger anxiety. This breed will also tend to be more anxious in general (if only slightly so) and will develop barking issues and other problematic habits faster than most dogs.

4: Jack Russell Terrier

These dogs are bundles of energy. They bore easily, and will need lots of entertainment and physical activity. If there is no human being close by to keep these dogs engaged and busy, things can quickly take a turn for the disastrous. And for a small dog; the Jack Russell Terrier is sure capable of a lot of damage.

5: German Shepherd

These canines are bred to work and remain physically "plugged-in" for most of the day. As such, they do best when in an environment that is both physically and mentally engaging. If left alone, they get bored quickly. They become distressed and shifty. Like the retriever; the breed has also experienced some health problems of late, and their worse temperament has them a lot more prone to distress.

6: Australian Shepherd

This dog is bred for herding. It is a very active dog and is at its best behavior when working. These dogs need to remain active; otherwise, they quickly develop anxiety when left with nothing to do.

7: Bichon Frise

This one is bred as a companion dog. This dog is really at its best when around its family. When left alone, it quickly becomes bored and may suffer severe anxiety disorder from loneliness.

8: Vizsla

These are hunting dogs, and they were primarily bred to hunt with their human buddies. They are very social in their own rugged way, and do very poorly when they are left alone. Living without much physical activity and being lonely most of the time will quickly lead to severe anxiety disorder.

9: German Shorthaired Pointer

This is yet another dog that was bred to hunt with his/her human friends. Since they are bred to be around people and stay physically engaged, they are quick to slide into anxiety when denied both factors.

10: Toy Poodle

This poodle has a gentle temperament, and has been bred for companionship. As such, it needs time and lots of love from its human family. When denied both of these; they suffer from considerable separation distress.

If you are on the lookout for a dog breed that is less prone to separation anxiety, you should consider the traditional Greyhound, the Basset hound, the Maltese and the French bulldog. The truth is that there are no dogs with zero separation anxiety issues. However, these breeds will be less likely to suffer from distress when left alone.

Let's take this discussion even further where part 2 of this book will focus on prevention of separation anxiety.

Part 2: Preventing Separation Anxiety In Dogs Before It Sets In

10 Potent Steps To Keep Separation Anxiety At Bay

The most vital ingredient to have in place, if your separation anxiety prevention program is to be successful, is to set up your furry friend for success from the word go.

Immediately you bring a new puppy or dog home, implement such a program as will help him or her be comfortable with spending time alone. Gradually increase the time periods that your dog is alone, eventually working up to the number of hours you typically expect him or her to be alone as the family leaves for work/school Etc. This will help him understand that you have not abandoned him; that you will come back, always.

Well, before you practice, make sure you exercise him properly. A dog that is exhausted and spent is a way better candidate for relaxation than one who is full of spunk and energy.

Here are 10 steps (of a program that should stretch to a couple of days), that will "create" a dog who is alright with being left home alone. Note that if you are trying to modify/eradicate a distress that is already existent, you will need to go through the steps outlined here a lot more slowly and patiently.

The Steps:

1: Bring the dog home at such a time when there is somebody who can spare a few days with him. This will help greatly ease the stress of transitioning.

2: Prepare a safe space for the dog in advance: a quiet, comfortable space such as a puppy pen or a play pen. You could also make a ready a dog-proofed room, with the laundry room being a proper candidate for this.

3: Once you bring your dog home, give him every chance to eliminate outdoors. Spend 10 to 15 minutes with the dog in the house and keep him under a vigilant eye. Afterward, you can place him in his pen and spend a few more minutes with him.

4: Stay close, at least at first. Read a book, go through your mail or something... just keep yourself busy and occupied. If your dog fusses; ignore him. When the dog falls quiet, greet him in a calm voice and then go back to what you were doing. You are basically teaching him that if you leave, he can expect you to return. Other members of the family should 'disappear' during this period of time: the dog needs to properly learn to be alone.

5: Continue stepping away occasionally. Gradually increase the distance as well as vary the time length that you are away from the dog. Eventually, you should be able to wander around the room without your dog getting overly excited or stimulated. Each time you return, greet him with a calm voice. Every now and then; say "yes!" in a cheerful but calm voice when you return. You can follow this up by walking to his pen and offering him a treat.

6: After about an hour or so, give the dog a break. Take him outdoors to either potty or play. You can hang out outdoors for a spell. After this, take him back inside and then resume his pen procedure.

7: Start again, but stay near his pen until he is settled. With more swiftness this time, move along both steps 4 and 5, until you can wander around the room without raising alarm in the dog. Now step into an adjacent room for a very brief moment of time and then return before the dog's upset. By and by, increase the amount of time that you are away from the room. Combine this with roaming around the room, taking a spot near him and reading your book and sitting some distance away from him reading your book. If he begins to fuss, wait until his tantrum is over and then move back to him. Teach the dog that a calm temperament will make you return and that fussing will ward you away.

8: On occasion, step outside your house. On the first day, your goal is to get your furry pet to be comfortable with your absence for 15-20 minutes. Usually, it's the first 20 minutes of absence that are the hardest to deal with. Vary the length of your absences so he doesn't start timing and anticipating your return. Remember that it is important that your dog has plenty of play and potty breaks… if you own a pup, take him out every hour. Older dogs can stay put for two hours.

9: On the 2nd day, swiftly go through the warm-up steps until you are able to step outside for 15-20 minutes without alarming your dog. Of course, you should be combining this with shorter absences. On one of your outdoor forays; hop into your car and drive around your block. Come back in about 10 minutes and re-enter your house calmly the same way you have during your prior separations. Hang out for a bit, and then hop onto your car and drive around for half an hour this time.

10: Now it is time for Sunday brunch. Make sure that your dog has a thorough break and playtime. Afterward, give him 15 minutes to stretch out and relax. Place a Kong that is filled with delightful doggy treats in his pen, round up your family and then exit the house calmly for a 3-hour long excursion. When you come back home to a contented, happy dog; you can celebrate your dog's graduation, from the separation anxiety prevention college.

Time alone for the dog: there are limits to this stuff

It is really unfair to ask a puppy to stay home alone for, say, 5-10 hours. The pup needs multiple potty breaks... hourly breaks, even. If you force the pup to soil indoors, you may well trigger stress-relative behavior. At the very least, you will be making it difficult for the dog to ever become properly housetrained.

Next, we will be focusing on how to treat separation anxiety.

Part 3: Effectively Treating Separation Anxiety In Dogs

How Do I Help My Dog? The Four Options Of Treating Separation Anxiety

Treating separation anxiety takes a lot of hard work. It is easy enough to get frustrated with your canine's destructive behavior... but remember; your dog is not making a calculated choice, with malicious intentions in mind.

He or she is panicked about survival without you. Your dog views you as, among other things, his or her pack. You offer company, love, protection, friendship, assurance, Etc. You are pretty much your dog's emotional, even physical anchor. When you are gone, a massive part of his world leaves with you. And seeing as dogs, like most animals, live in the moment; it becomes easy enough to succumb to feelings of loneliness and terror. Your dog genuinely believes he is abandoned.

Have this in mind as you prepare to make the necessary steps to cure your dog's separation anxiety. It will help you be that much more patient and understanding.

There are some who believe that part of effectively conditioning dogs involves a bit of whipping. The thing is... you will never properly cure your dog's separation anxiety if you keep reaching for sticks. All you will succeed in doing is intimidating him. By and by, the very same issues will crop up again.

With this in mind, these are the viable options in helping your dog and curing his or her separation anxiety:

1. **Conditioning**: Conditioning your dog works in that the procedures involved are hinged on having your dog understand that separation has its own rewards. Your dog is conditioned to immediately flip into stress mode when he or she understands you are leaving. One of the more basic counters is to leave the dog some treat or other, say, a toy stuffed with peanut butter or a bone to gnaw on. You can even leave treats strewn around the house for him or her to discover. (If your dog's a pup; it is smart to condition him as early as possible, making sure you leave him alone for increasingly longer time periods. Basically, the steps outlined in the previous chapter will suffice. Consider too, that some dogs will feel significantly safer and more comfortable when left in their crate, as opposed to having the entire house opened up for them to roam free. Observe your dog closely when you place him in a crate and see what his reactions are.)

Conditioning is, by some distance, the most intensive of all treatment strategies. As such, most of this section's meat, pun unintended, will concentrate on it. However, for conditioning to work with maximum effectiveness, it is necessary to combine it with other strategies such as exercise.

2. **Exercise**: Exercise is a very effective strategy in curing separation anxiety... so much so, that lots of dogs have

registered far less destructive tendencies when exercise alone was added to their daily routine. Ensure that your dog gets enough exercise, both in a physical and mental capacity. When your dog is spent and contented; he will be a lot more likely to settle down and nap when you leave.

3. **Medication**: Sometimes, no amount of conditioning and training will work. This is especially true with older dogs. This is where medication comes in. There are vets who recommend such medication as amitriptyline, which is quite effective at treating depression. Alprazolam is yet another; which is prescribed for anxiety as well as other panic disorders. They will be covered concisely in a separate chapter.

4. **Herbal and homeopathic treatments**: Yet another option involves natural supplements and homeopathic treatment. Some natural supplements that will help liftoff the anxiety your dog suffers when you leave are inclusive of the amino acid L Theanine, passionflower, chamomile, valerian and St. John's Wort. Basically, they function as neurotransmitters in the dog's brain, inducing a sense of calm and peace. This will be covered in ample detail in a chapter of its own.

Where Do I Start? Creating A Suitable Environment & Routine For Your Dog

The previous chapter outlined the treatment strategies for separation anxiety. It also highlighted that conditioning will take up most of this section of the book, as it is by far the most varied and intensive strategy. As such, even as you go ahead and attempt to create the most suitable environment and routine for your shaggy pal, what you are effectively doing is ensuring that the conditioning procedures will flow in the most efficient manner once you get to them. In fact, creating a suitable environment and a proper routine is, in itself, conditioning work.

Before we dip into the steps of our subject matter; let's dedicate a few sentences to rewards.

Rewards

Rewards will make or break your effectiveness in conditioning your dog and effectively clearing separation anxiety. If you're messy in how you bestow rewards, your dog won't make requisite correlations regarding the rewards and the behavior that brought them about. Your dog, predictably, will have much harder time learning. Ensure that all rewards are identified; that they are only given for behaviors you are deliberately training. Never reward attention-seeking behavior in the dog, or else he'll just be more motivated to trash your house when you are away.

1. Establish a routine that is predictable and uncomplicated

Even in human beings, predictable patterns are sure-fire bringers of calm and peace. This is even more so in dogs, who literally live in the moment and rely way more heavily on instinct than calculated thought.

Your dog is anxious. As such, your very first step to making him calm is by making his day predictable. This is whether you are spending time at home or have to leave. Establish a routine where your dog will easily begin to predict when he can expect attention/human presence. This is inclusive of feeding, exercise, play, training and elimination.)

Establish a routine where he is conditioned for inattention (be it napping, being left alone with his choice toys, Etc.) Of course, it will help a great deal if you schedule the latter times at times when you expect to leave the house.

2. Environmental enrichment- meeting the needs of your dog

It is important that you thoroughly squeeze out everything and cover all the bases during those times when you interact with your dog. By the time you're done, your dog should crave a nice, long nap more than anything else. Make sure you meet all his needs: exercise him properly, train him, make sure he eliminates, and others. Naturally, you can't cover all of these bases in one block of time. Even if you could, your dog couldn't. Have several, regular interactive sessions that ensure your dog is subject to sufficient attention and play.

If your breed of dog is the sort that is very high energy; you can provide novel, motivational toys for him to play with when your sessions are done. Chew toys are great, for example.

3. Establish a predictable reward protocol

A lot of time, if not most of the time, if your dog suffers from separation anxiety; it is very likely that your dog's preferred rewards are the play and attention that you provide. As such, foods, treats, chew toys and play may be highly desirable for him.

Start out by asking yourself this: What behavior does my dog need learning, and what set of behaviors must I never reinforce?

With separation anxiety, you want to reinforce your dog settling down, being and staying relaxed, showing some degree of independence, etc. Attention seeking and following behaviors must not be reinforced. As such, training needs to focus on relaxed and extended down-stays, as well as going to a mat or bed on command. After enough time has passed, you can give attention and affection as a reward. By and by; shape longer time periods of distance and inattention before closeness and affection is given. The goal, it perhaps needs saying, is not to ignore the dog. Rather, it is to ignore attention seeking behavior. You are keen on ensuring your dog learns that calm and peaceable behavior is the only way he gets your attention.

4. Train "settle"

The training goal is to have your dog learn to settle comfortably on cue. Before you give him any reward, focus on having him in a settled-down position, or perhaps lying on his mat or bed. Not only must you ignore attention-seeking behavior and tantrums; all casual interactions must be eschewed for the first several weeks. You need to make it crystal clear to your dog that settling down draws rewards and attention-seeking only pushes you away.

Practice down-stays using food lures, head halter training or clicker training. By and by, shape longer times on the mat or bed before you give attention, treats and play.

5. Develop an area and surface for relaxing

Remember, establishing predictability will get you further. Having a mat or bed location, say in a room, crate or pen, where the dog can be taught to rest, take naps, play with toys and even sleep, will provide a secure, familiar area where the dog may settle when you leave.

It will be a safe, fun space. You may start by training the dog to go to the area and then gradually shape increasingly longer stays as well as more relaxed responses in this area before you give any rewards. It may also be greatly helpful to have in place a barricade, a tie-down or a crate that is easily closed to ensure the dog stays in its area long enough each session before release. On the other hand, you need to know what your dog's limits are. Your dog needs to be calm and settled at the time of release, and not a baying, whimpering wreck. This is necessary so you completely avoid reinforcing crying/barking behavior.

At first, you can take your dog to this area using a treat or toy as a lure. You may even do this using a leash or head halter. In time, a daily routine ought to be established, where the dog knows to lie on his bed/mat after each session of exercise, play and training. He can mess around with his toys or take a nap... he just has to be settled on his mat. This is very similar to crate-training, where the dog's mat or bed becomes its playpen.

Other than having sessions of play, exercise and training in this particular area, ensure your dog receives some or all of his rewards in this area only. Such audible cues as radio or TV, odors such as aromatherapy-candles and pieces of clothing with your scent; and a reasonably comfortable bed will help promote a relaxed response, seeing as they are associated with relaxation and your presence.

6. Work on responses to simple commands

For some dogs, it is necessary to have them effectively earn all things. This may be as simple as having your dog respond to such commands as "sit" before he gets what he's after. For instance, if your dog wants to go outside, you can instruct him to "sit" prior to opening the door. Once he complies, you can open the door.

You can use this technique for anything he desires.

Buckling Down: Effective, Responsive Conditioning Measures To Cure Separation Anxiety In Your Dog

By this point, you are handily equipped with routines, procedures, responses and preparations for separation anxiety.

Even if you were to put the book down and not proceed past this point, you'd likely do more than a passable job at alleviating separation anxiety. Still, it is important that you understand exactly what to do in response to potential situations your dog may put both of you in.

Because for sure, it may not be enough to just have the right environment in place as well as take preventive measures. It could be that your dog's problems run deeper than you thought... it could be that your dog has spent time in abusive conditions in the past, and you thus require doing more.

In this chapter, which will be the longest of them all; we will amply cover conditioning your dog to alleviate separation anxiety, but in a Q&A format. By the very end, we will have covered every base and angle that needs covering, as well as provided well-fleshed out answers and solutions.

Without further ado:

1. When I need to leave the house, what could I do immediately to prevent damage and house-trashing?

This is a difficult question... extremely so. Your ultimate goal is to reduce the dog's anxiety level by having him or her feel comfortable and calm in your absence.

This can be a lengthy process.

Yet, most owners shall need to deal with vocalization or damage immediately.

Let us examine your options in this regard:

During the initial retraining, it may be very necessary to acquire the services of a dog sitter. You may have to have your dog accompany you to work, find a trustworthy friend to dog-sit, perhaps board him/her for the day or even arrange for time off from work for proper retraining.

Crate training and dog proofing methods may work well, especially if you've already trained your dog to "operate" in a specific, confined area (like the previous chapter recommends). Still, you need to be wary as far as crates go. If a dog has a severe case of separation anxiety; it is entirely likely that he'll badly injure himself as he intensely attempts to escape the crate's confinement.

It is vital that you choose a room that will not further spike the dog's anxiety. Your dog's feeding place or bedroom is, thus, the most practical option. Booby traps may be effective in keeping the dog off of potential problem areas.

For vocalization; anti-bark devices may be effective in the short term. The problem here is that anti-bark devices do nothing to reduce anxiety. And for some dogs, the urge to vocalize may be far too strong for these devices to succeed in much more than hurting the dog.

Anti-anxiety drugs and pheromones might be useful, at least until such a time when you have effectively conditioned your dog to be calm in your absence.

2. What should I do before departures?

As a rule of thumb, make sure that before any lengthy departure, you provide a vigorous exercise and play session. We've mentioned this in passing, in previous chapters. The aim is to tire him or her out as well as provide an ample period of attention. You're killing two birds with one stone.

A training session may be a productive way to interact further with your dog and 'work' with him or her. For the final 15-30 minutes before you leave, your dog must be ignored. It would be even better if you took your dog to rest in a relaxation area that has a TV, radio or even a video set to playback (we recommended this, in passing, in the previous chapter.) You can then prepare to leave while the dog is both out of sight and earshot.

At this point, provide the dog with new, motivational toys so that he or she is occupied and sufficiently distracted both before and during your departure. The key is avoiding as many of the usual departure cues as you can, so that the dog's anxiety isn't spiked just before you leave.

Brushing your teeth, getting into work gear, collecting your keys, putting things in the purse/briefcase, Etc., are all things that you can do away from the dog's line of sight. You may even consider changing clothes at work and even preparing and packing your lunch the previous night to further avoid alerting your dog on your departure. You could even leave your car at your neighbor's so the dog won't hear the car pulling out.

Avoid saying goodbye, as this will only bring attention to your departure. Yet another tactic is to expose your dog to as many departure cues (picking up keys, packing your briefcase, getting into work gear) as possible while intending to go nowhere. By and by, they will no longer be predictive of your departure.

3. What do I do if I come home to an unholy mess?

If your dog has been anxious when you were away, and this has led to destruction, soiling or a combination of both; anything you do immediately may only succeed in heightening the dog's anxiety. This will only make matters worse in the future, and will not correct what's already been done. Thus, you must avoid both punishment as well as excited greetings. When you get home, ignore the dog until he or she settles down. This may take the better part of a quarter hour. Your dog will soon learn that the faster she settles, and the calmer she gets; the sooner your attention comes.

4. What may be done to reduce anxiety during departure time?

As you leave, the dog should be kept busy and occupied. Preferably, he or she should be out of sight and earshot. This will help reduce anxiety. Handing the dog special treats that are primarily saved for departures and for down-stay exercises may help keep the dog distracted – perhaps even having fun – while you leave. Dogs which are highly aroused by food may well be so intensely occupied by a peanut butter-coated toy, a fresh rawhide piece, a toy stuffed with liver or frozen treats that they may only notice you've left a long time after the fact. Make sure that the distraction devices can last for as long as possible, as this will ensure your dog will be distracted until you have long gone.

For instance, frozen treats placed in the dog's bowl; toys tightly stuffed with goodies; toys designed to require work and manipulation for the food reward inside to be obtained; toys that can withstand maintained chewing and timer-feeders which open throughout the day etc. are solid suggestions.

Determine what motivates your dog best. For instance, if a specific toy captures the dog's attention way more than other toys do, have two more in place, rather than providing toys that are less effective at occupying the dog.

It may also help to provide the dog some or all of its food with several special surprises at the bowl bottom. On rare occasions, a second pet may help occupy the dog and have him or her sufficiently distracted when leaving.

5. Way before I'm even prepared to leave, my dog is already anxious and fretting. What can I do?

If this is the case with your dog, then you definitely are guilty of stacking up cues that you are leaving even before you are actually prepared to. This is the only logical reason, seeing as dogs don't own predictive crystal balls. There are activities that you may often do that preface leaving the house. If, for example, you like to boil a great big pot of coffee an hour before you leave, your dog is going to begin associating your humming coffee maker as an early precursor of leaving. If you like to trot around the house, toothbrush in mouth, multi-tasking as you prepare to depart; your dog will very quickly put two and two together. Dogs are intelligent this way.

However, you can use this to your advantage. Dogs are also capable of learning signals that communicate that you are not intending to leave, thus enabling them to relax.

Thus, you can either take away all activities that are potential cues (and perform them away from the dog) or you can retrain the dog that these cues are no longer precursors for leaving the house. However, understand that some dogs are extremely intelligent. Despite your best efforts, they may still be able to accurately decipher some activities as cues for leaving. Train the dog to associate such activities with situations of relaxation and enjoyment. A good way to do this is to perform all these activities after you arrive home, or on weekend mornings when you intend to go nowhere... run the coffee maker but then proceed to spend the rest of the day with your canine. Etc.

Get your usual departure gear –keys, briefcase, shoes, overcoat and the like – and walk to the door. However, do not exit. Your dog will be watching you closely… he may even get up. Once you put away these things however, he will lie down again. Once the dog is calm, repeat the baiting process. Only perform 3 to 4 reps a day and ensure that the dog is cool and quiet before you repeat. This is to discourage attention-seeking behavior. Eventually, the dog will learn to ignore these cues, as they're "non-threatening". This way, your dog will be a lot less anxious when you exit the house.

6. What can I do to retrain my dog to reduce both dependence and following?

The most vital element of retraining is to teach the dog to practice independence and relaxation in your presence. Only when the dog stays in his relaxation area or bed, will you be ready to start mock departures.

You must ensure that attention seeking behavior is never rewarded. Any attempts at seeking attention, no matter how concerted, must be met with aloof indifference. On the other hand, calm behavior needs rewarding. Teach the dog that rewards and attention will only be forthcoming if he calms down, lies in his area and stops following you around and whining.

Teach the dog to calm down and relax in his relaxation area, and to be content with long periods of inattention when you are at home. Of course, you may have to start with shorter spans of inattention and gradually graduate to longer spells. Training will be a lot quicker and more efficient if the dog learns the down stay on command. Make sure that you schedule attention, play and interaction sessions and then develop a routine while at home. Follow these with increasingly longer sessions of inattention and aloofness (for playing with toys and napping) in an attempt to approximate your departure times. The dog, by and by, will get used to the routine in place so that you can leave the house while he's calm.

7. Beyond using mock departures and cue-retraining, how can I outright teach my dog to accept my departures?

Formal training should be primarily focused on having the dog stay on his mat, in bed or in his crate/den area. He should be made to do so for increasingly longer time periods. It may be necessary to start with food lure exercises, beginning with a down stay and then gradually increasing the time and level of relaxation in each session.

Once your dog "stays" in your presence, start to walk away and then return, starting with a few feet for a few seconds and then progressing over time. Eventually, you should be leaving the room for 30 minutes plus and returning without much fuss. Reward the dog with an attention session, perhaps getting back and giving him a massage or a gentle tummy rub.

This way, you shape and reinforce the desired behavior with the attention he so desires. However, remember that attention, at times, especially on demand, will encourage the dog to fret, follow and pester rather than calm down in his area. A head halter is your friend throughout training, to ensure the dog remains in position and promptly responds to commands.

From this point going forward, the dog should be encouraged to stay in his crate or bed for extended time periods as opposed to sitting at your feet or your lap. If the dog can be trained to sleep in his area of relaxation at night rather than your bed/bedroom, this may be very effective in breaking over-attachment and dependence quickly. During the exercises, use as many cues as you can to have the dog relax. Mimic the secure, unthreatening environment that the dog feels when you are home. Leave your TV on. Play some music, or a favorite video. Leave him a favorite blanket or one of his favored chew toys. All of these cues will be quite effective at relaxing your dog and helping him stay calm and accept your departures.

8. How do I progress to actually leaving the house... and having my dog remain unperturbed?

During your mock departures (discussed in the previous point), make sure that your dog is exercised, made to go through a short training session and then taken to his bed to relax. Give your dog the down stay command, a few treats and toys and then exit when the dog is both distracted and relaxed.

The first few mock departures must be identical to the training exercises that we have been discussing all through this chapter (especially in the retraining paragraphs). But instead of just leaving the scene and moving to a different room; you will begin to exit the home altogether. The first departures ought to just be long enough to leave the home and return before the dog begins to feel anxious and fret. These sessions may only last several minutes at most. The most critical part will for sure be exiting the front door without arousing the dog and stoking the fires of anxiety. Gradually, but in a random manner, increase the time periods that you are gone. When you begin a session, your dog must be in a calm state to ensure that you do not mistakenly reward attention seeking behavior.

Your departures must be simulated to resemble real ones as closely as possible. Perform all activities that you would normally do when leaving... while you may have successfully retrained your canine to not associate your briefcase and keys with leaving; there's only so much you can do with opening and closing your car door, turning on the engine, Etc. Your dog will, at least on some level, associate these with departure, since they will often be the last things he hears before you actually leave. However, you can still retrain him to a level where he at least understands there is a high potential of your departures only being short lived, as far as these sounds and activities are concerned. Behave as though you are actually leaving… start the engine, rev it up, and pull the car out of the driveway and return. Repeat this several times, making sure to randomly vary the time periods you are gone. The idea is to not settle into some easily readable pattern. This way, your dog will come to repeatedly believe that your departures always have the potential to be short, and that even if they're not; you will for sure still show up.

Speaking of departures involving cars…

9. Why is it that my dog is all up in arms when I leave home… but is cool as a cucumber when I leave the car?

Many dogs that wreck the home when left alone will docilely stay in a van or car without showing any anxiety or destructive habits. A major reason is that the dog has learned to lean back and enjoy car rides without being subject to much physical attention and contact. And when you do exit the car, your departures almost always tend to be short-lived. As such, it will usually be possible to leave the dog in the car for actual long time periods without stoking any anxiety. This provides a degree of proof that the dog can learn to relax and let his hair down if he gets used to being ignored, and is in a location where he genuinely feels settled, and gets acquainted with departures on a gradual basis. This is very similar to the way in which the dog ought to be trained to relax at home, and gradually come to terms with longer departures.

10. Is drug therapy truly effective?

Yes, drug therapy may be useful, especially during the initial stages of departure training. However, tranquilizers alone will not cut down on your dog's anxiety, and may only be useful in sedating the dog so that he's less likely to run amok and wreck the house. This is not to mean that he actually won't do it... but it may help to at least minimize the ends to which he'll go to "escape" his isolation.

Most dogs tend to do best with either clomipramine or fluoxetine, applied over several months. These may be combined with other anti-anxiety drugs if necessary.

Although drugs may be vital in cutting down on your dog's underlying anxiety and helping him cope better, the real deal is the retraining program that you put your dog through. This is why this chapter places so much emphasis on activities to do to both train and retrain your dog to deal with isolation.

Teaching your dog independence and relaxation in your absence is the real victory. Drugs and sedation must only come in as a last resort. However, if you feel that you require drugs to help you handle your dog's separation anxiety issues; reach out to a vet and discuss potential options. Do not make the mistake of just buying drugs over the counter and hoping they work.

How To Treat and Prevent Separation Anxiety In Dogs

Here is an important resource that discusses medication for separation anxiety in dogs, with effective drug examples: https://shopus.furbo.com/blogs/guide-to-helping-dogs-with-separation-anxiety/chapter-2-medication-for-separation-anxiety

With these 10 all-comprehensive steps, you are more than sufficiently armed with techniques and strategies to treat your dog's separation anxiety.

Here are some other avenues to explore, to complement your modification work:

- Exercise the dog properly before leaving. This has been discussed multiple times in this book already. A tired dog will have a lot less energy with which it can transform to anxiety and destruction. End the exercise sessions about 20-30 minutes before departing, so that he has ample time to settle down and get distracted.

- Five minutes before leaving, give your doggy a well-stuffed Kong so that he's sufficiently distracted from your imminent departure.

- Make departures and returns absolutely calm and lacking in emotion. No cushy/kissy "papa loves you" stuff. If your dog gets all excited and leaps all over you upon returning, ignore him, inasmuch as you want to respond to his affections. Give him your back and stroll away. When the dog finally calms and settles down; say your hello and then greet him calmly.

- Defuse pieces of departure routine so disqualify them as cues. You do this by also performing them when there is no intention of actually leaving. Pick up the car keys and then sit on your sofa and watch TV. Dress in business attire and proceed to cook your dinner. Set the alarm for 5.30 a.m. on Saturday, and then roll over on your side and get back to your sleep.

- Mix up pieces of the usual departure routine and activities when you do not intend to leave at all, so that his anxiety does not build up to a fever pitch. If he can read and recognize departure cues with successive days of accuracy, it will be easier for him to go straight into anxiety mode when he reads them. Man is a habit-oriented creature too; so this will be hard enough to do. However, it can pay off massively if you pull it off. Eat your breakfast just before you shower, rather than having it after you shower. Pick up the car keys and then put them in the coat pocket just before taking your canine out for his last potty break. Take your briefcase and put it in your car but instead of doing this in your work attire, do it in lounging shorts or your pajamas. The idea is to make your morning as unreadable as possible from your dog's perspective.

- Use such "safe" cues as "I'll be back soon," only in those times when you know you will be back within a time period that the dog can easily tolerate. As is suggested in author Patricia McConnell's phenomenal book on treating separation anxiety, titled "I'll Be Home Soon"; this will help the dog relax, as he knows full well that he can expect you to imminently return.

- Explore other varied dog-keeping situations so as to minimize occasions when you really do have to go and leave him on his own for a long time period: doggie daycare, for example, may be great for some dogs. However, it is a poor option for other dogs. You can also consider a neighbor or a relative who works at home and would appreciate the company of your dog.

- If you get to a point where you consider adopting a second dog to help out with loneliness; try and settle for a dog that is calm and stable. You want a compatible companion to your dog so that even in the event of anxiety, the companion's presence helps to quickly dissipate it.

Finally, we will discuss how to use herbal remedies to fight separation anxiety in dogs.

Homeopathic And Herbal Remedies For Separation Anxiety In Your Dog

Pulsatilla nigicans (Pasque-flower)

This stands as one most commonly administered homeopathic medicines given to remedy separation anxiety. It should be administered in either the 6c or 30c. You can give it orally to your dog or you can add it to the dog's water throughout the day. As we've already said, you must only resort to medicines as a last resort, and retraining your dog is where it really is at.

However, if the issues are too deep-rooted and there's some obvious trauma or other boiling underneath, you can consider this medicine.

Calcarea phosphorica (Calcium Phosphate)

This is yet another beneficial medicine that is used to remedy separation anxiety. It is best used in either the 6c or 30c potency. This remedy is best suited for dogs that are especially destructive, and are wrecking things left and right and chewing through furniture. If your dog is especially over-attached and gets overly upset when left alone, this one will be ideal. "Calc Phos" is also effective at calming down dogs that have a hard time during storms. If your dog trembles and shakes when thunder is rolling, this homeopathic medicine will help him pipe down and stay docile.

Gelsemium (Yellow Jasmine)

Animals that require *Gelsemium* are referred to as "tremblers." With "Yellow Jasmine dogs", there is considerable quivering, and this can range from a singular muscle group to the dog's entire body. In instances where, even after intensive retraining efforts, your dog still gets so worked up that it develops diarrhea and/or involuntary urination when left alone, Yellow Jasmine will be a major help.

Passiflora (Passion flower)

This one is a calming anti-convulsant. It slows down or "depresses" the dog's entire nervous system. The good thing with this homeopathic medicine is that it is very swift acting and is also non-addictive. You can administer it either in tincture form or added to the dog's daily water.

Scutellaria (Skullcap) and *Valerian*

These herbal medicines are wonderful remedies that offer swift symptomatic relief in the case of extreme anxiety and nervousness.

Kava Kava

Kava Kava is a traditional herb that is used in Polynesian ceremonies. It is phenomenal in reducing anxiety, relaxing tension (inclusive of muscle tension), and it calms restlessness without necessarily sacrificing mental sharpness. *Kava kava* is a great choice if you have a dog that will just not calm down when you prepare to depart. It is available in multiple forms: capsule, powdered, tincture, and ground. Both the ground and powdered kava kava forms can be either made into "kava tea" or added to your dog's daily water. You may also sprinkle it into food.

These are, by some distance, the most common and effective natural remedies in use today for separation anxiety. They have been amply tried and tested, and have been in use for many years already. Today, there are numerous toxic drugs available on the market. Most of these will have labels that claim to aid your dog calm down but in truth, most of them come with far too many side effects to be sufficiently beneficial to your dog.

Conclusion

As far as separation anxiety guides go, this one is peerless. Rather than merely shove solutions in your face from the off, this guide takes you through the dog's own psyche, helping you understand why he behaves the way he does. The ultimate theme here is patience, as well as making sure to effectively weed out attention seeking behavior in the dog before hoping to see results. Remember – your dog is not trying to wind you up when he or she breaks furniture and perhaps wrecks the rugs: the dog's actions are coming from a place of genuine fear and anxiety. Be patient and steadily work on retraining him so that he's calm when you are away. If you keep at it, it will only be a matter of time before you succeed.

Do You Like My Book & Approach To Publishing?

If you like my writing and style and would love the ease of learning literally everything you can get your hands on from Fantonpublishers.com, I'd really need you to do me either of the following favors.

1: First, I'd Love It If You Leave a Review of This Book on Amazon.

2: Get Updates When I Publish New Books

Visit my Amazon page and subscribe to receive notifications whenever I publish new books.

Check out my dog training books:

Dog Tricks: 15 Tricks You Must Teach Your Dog before Anything Else by Bruno Michael

Dog Separation Anxiety: How To Treat And Prevent Separation Anxiety In Dogs by Bruno Michael

Dog Barking Excessively?: How to Get Your Dog to Stop Barking Excessively

DOG NUTRITION by Bruno Michael

3: Grab Some Freebies On Your Way Out; Giving Is Receiving, Right?

I gave you a complimentary book at the start of the book. If you are still interested, grab it here.

[5 Pillar Life Transformation Checklist](http://bit.ly/2fantonfreebie): http://bit.ly/2fantonfreebie